THE
REDTHROATS

DAVID CALE

VINTAGE BOOKS

A Division of Random House
New York

A Vintage Original, January 1989

FIRST EDITION

Cale, David.
  The redthroats.
  "A Vintage original."
  Contents: The redthroats—Smooch music.
  I. Title. II. Title: Smooch music.
PR6053.A379R44 1989   822'.914   88-40054
ISBN 0-679-73961-0 (pbk.)

Photographs on pages 9, 25, and 37 by Paula Court; photographs on pages 55, 77, and 87 by Jay Thompson.

Manufactured in the United States of America
10 9 8 7 6 5 4 3 2 1

"With a sleek, almost parsimonious peak of details, Cale manages to transform [his] strange but ordinary [characters] into hero-victims of a hopeless contemporary landscape."
—*The Chicago Tribune*

"Inspired by his own childhood, Cale weaves black humor with distinctive surreal imagery to an effect that's both painful and beguiling."
—*Vogue*

"He is an original. His point of view is unique, always angst-ridden, insightful and never less than compelling."
—*Los Angeles Herald Examiner*

"Captivating, disarming, filled with sweetness and wonderment . . . Cale's unerring eye for the offbeat detail and his uncomplaining acceptance of the inadvertency of events give *The Redthroats* the flavor of a storybook fable."
—*The Washington Post*

"Cale tales are as much fugue as drama . . . He weaves a yarn of the eerie and the bizarre. . . . You laugh, fear and take heart: He leaves you with energy and the catharsis of Aristotelian recognition."
—*L.A. Weekly*

"The tales he spins . . . distil the yearning inner lives of everyday people with a surreal intensity. Reality, fantasy and an almost clairvoyant insight into personality dissolve into one another in stories that can be as memorable as one's own most vivid dreams."
—*The New York Times*

ACKNOWLEDGMENTS

Many people have shown me support and encouragement. In particular I would like to thank my editor, Julie Grau, and David Rosenthal at Random House.

Special thanks also to Mark Amitin, Bill Barnes, C. Carr, Paula Court, Ray Dobbins, Simon Egleton, Richard Elovich, Gustavo Gonzalez, Sabrina Hamilton, Signe Hammer, Amy Heller, Stephen Holden, Holly Hughes, Brad Jones, Paul Lawrence, Scott Macaulay, Carol McDowell, Russell Metheny, Roy Nathanson, Kate Nelligan, Madeline Puzo, David Richards, E.J. Rodriguez, Alison Rooney, Mark Russell, the New York State Council on the Arts, the New York Foundation for the Arts and the Kitchen's Touring Program.

CONTENTS

THE REDTHROATS

For Barbara Arnold

A NOTE ON THE PERFORMANCE OF THE REDTHROATS

The Redthroats is performed on a bare stage with a single chair and no props.

An old man standing next to a river in Liddleton

It was a little river that ran through the town. Only about ten inches deep. The water was kind of dirty. There were fish in the river but it was hard to locate them on account of all the muck. In the summer you'd see groups of kids going down the hill with green nylon nets. You could buy the nets at the newspaper shop. They'd all be wearing Wellington boots. You'd see them step into the river with their little green nets to catch fish. Minnows mostly. The odd gudgeon. Occasionally a newt, and sometimes a redthroat. Now redthroats were the most highly prized. The kids always kept them. They were these little fish with stickles on their backs. From above they seemed quite dull but if you looked underneath they

5

had a bright red patch between the mouth and the gills. It would go real quiet, then all of a sudden you'd hear,

"Redthroat! Redthroat! I've got a redthroat!"

And there'd be a lot of splashing around in the river as the kids ran to examine the little fish.

Now catching redthroats was a double-edged thing. There was a danger involved on account of the fact that the redthroats liked to frequent the area of water next to the bridge, which was also the haunt of the leeches. Kids were always half terrified a leech was going to climb up into their Wellington boot and suck all the blood out of their foot. But this just made the redthroats all the more valuable. Kids would stand in the river all day sometimes, just waiting for redthroats.

Then one day the redthroats disappeared. Nobody could work out where they'd gone to. They just went away.

1

THE WEIRDS

Steven at 11

Once upon a time there was a town called Liddleton in which all the people worked in factories. And living in Liddleton was a strange family who never left the town, not even to visit somewhere else: THE WEIRDS.

Mrs. Weird was agitated. Well, Mrs. Weird was always agitated, but today she was especially edgy. She paced the kitchen like a cat in a cage. She slapped her hand down on the sink. Then she began to scream at Mr. Weird,

"Steven spends too much time in his room with those damn Judy Garland records! He should be getting out. Out and about. Doing boys' things. He should be fixing cars. He should be collecting cigarette cards. He should be playing pranks on people! Are you

listening to me? Are you hearing what I'm saying?
It's not healthy, an eleven-year-old boy listening to
a dead woman sing!"

Mr. Weird didn't say anything. He just got up from the table
and went into the next room.

"It's not healthy,"
cried Mrs. Weird.
"It's not healthy!"

But young Steven was happiest when he was listening to Judy
Garland sing. Or to be more accurate, when he was actually
singing along with Judy, whether it be at The Palace or at
Carnegie Hall.

"Forget your troubles
And just get happy,
You better throw all your cares away.
Sing hallelujah,
Come on get happy,
Get ready for the judgment day.
Sun is shining,
Come on get happy,
The Lord is waiting to take your hand.
Shout hallelujah,
Come on get happy,
We're going to be going to the promised land.
We're heading 'cross a river,
Wash your sins away in the tide.
It's oh so peaceful on the other side.
Forget your troubles

"It's not healthy, an eleven-year-old boy listening to a dead woman sing!"

And just get happy,
You better throw all your cares away.
Sing hallelujah,
Come on get happy,
Get ready,
Get ready,
Get ready,
For the judgment day!"

"I wish he'd shut up singing. I can't hear my program.
He's drowning the TV,"

thought Mr. Weird and he got up to go and say something
but then he thought no, and flopped back down on the couch
and fell asleep. But while he was sleeping he was releasing gas.

"Peeeooooooooh! Ron!"

cried Mrs. Weird when she came into the room to wake him up.

"You're ruining the couch!
Smell gets into furniture and stays there.
I don't want a couch that stinks every time you sit on it.
I'll never have a home."

"I can't help it,"

said Mr. Weird.

"It's nature."

"It's not nature. It's disgusting. It ruins couches. And
you've got dirt on the Oriental rug, from the bottom
of your shoes. Look at this dirt. My rug! Your shoes!"

Mrs. Weird dived down onto the Oriental rug.

"You're ruining the rug. It takes two Chinese children three weeks to sew one square inch of one of

these carpets. All so you can wipe your filthy feet
all over it? Those children die before they reach fifteen. You're ruining the only evidence that they ever
existed. I'll never have anything."

Mr. Weird looked at the carpet but he couldn't see any dirt.
Mrs. Weird was always seeing dirt that wasn't there. Imaginary dirt. She has this thing about imaginary dirt, he thought,
but he didn't say anything. He didn't want to make more
trouble.

"Why can't I have a home like ordinary people?
Why do I have to have a pigsty?
Other people's families aren't like this family.
Why can't I have a family like other people?
Why can't I have a lovely home like other people?
Why don't you talk to me instead of watching TV?
Why don't you talk to me instead of never being home?
Why don't you talk to me instead of always being asleep?
Why don't you look at me when I'm talking to you!"

The main love of Mr. Weird's life was his extensive collection
of sparkling wines of the world. In the morning before Mrs.
Weird was awake he'd slip into the bathroom with a cup of
sparkling wine and sit on the toilet sipping it. In the bathroom
he could forget the outside world. There were no pressures
in the bathroom. The bathroom was like a pink cocoon. A
tiled womb in which to retreat. Sometimes he'd be in there
for hours just drinking wine, and reading soft-core porno-
graphic magazines which he kept under the carpet.

"Now, slave, you have thirty lashes left to be given as punishment. You will be punished by giving me pleasure at the same time. You will lick my feet when I order you to and the more you please me, the less strokes you will get. You will still get all thirty, but some strokes will be more painful than others, depending on how well you please me. Now lick my feet, slave. Lick my feet."

Mrs. Weird banged on the door.

"What are you doing? You've been in the bathroom forty-five minutes. What are you doing in there? What is your problem?"

"'Ugh!"
cried Mr. Weird.

And he panicked and tried to flush *OUCH* down the toilet.

Now young Steven kept birds. Two birds. Two canaries in a cage. All day long they would whistle and sing to their hearts' content. He had to get male canaries because female canaries don't sing. But even though they were male Steven called them Judy and Liza. The only trouble with Judy and Liza was that they were messy feeders. Threw their food all over the place.

"Birdseed! Birdseed! Everywhere you walk there's birdseed!"
cried Mrs. Weird when she walked across the kitchen to make breakfast.

"Why do I have to live with birdseed?
Bloody canaries."

Steven could hear her shouting so he didn't come out of his room, even though it did mean missing his Cocoa Crispies. Mrs. Weird carried on, shouting to herself,

"Why can't you hang clothes up? What do you think clothes hangers are for? Decoration?"

Mr. Weird came downstairs sheepishly.

"And what time did you roll in last night?
Well? Well? Well, here's your dinner."

Mrs. Weird yanked open the oven door and pulled out Mr. Weird's dinner. It was so dried up it didn't even look like food anymore.

"I spend hours slaving over a chicken cacciatore. All because I know how much you love my chicken cacciatore. All so you can let it shrivel up to nothing just sitting there in the oven waiting for you to eat it? I try to please you and what does it get me? What? A headache from tension and a dried-out bird. I give up."

Mrs. Weird clutched her head. Mr. Weird didn't say anything. He just went into the next room and put on his working clothes.

Now Mr. and Mrs. Weird made hats. Ladies' hats. Ladies' hats for every occasion. Weddings. Bar mitzvahs. Hats for funerals. Hats to be fashionable in. Hats to go horse racing.

13

Every day the Weirds would get in the car, drive to the hat factory and make hats.

The man who owned the factory was Mr. Weird's father. Hiss! He didn't like Mrs. Weird. Didn't think she was good enough for his family so he was always mean to her. Like he thought that if he were mean enough, she'd just go away. He'd pick on her all day and make her do all the nasty jobs that nobody else wanted to do. Mr. Weird was frightened of him because, although he was only a little man, he had a big temper. Whenever Mr. Weird did anything wrong he'd call him "idiot!" In front of everyone he'd say, "You idiot! You're an idiot!" Which only made Mr. Weird make more mistakes and that just made his father call him "idiot" even more.

Whenever he called him "idiot" poor Mr. Weird would run out and buy a glass of sparkling wine because he said it relaxed him. Sometimes he'd be in bars for hours—just relaxing, and swallowing Valium which he kept in an empty cigarette packet in his inside coat pocket.

"Where's that idiot son of mine?"

Mr. Weird's father would shout and he'd send one of the men to go out and find him. Well the men in the factory were mean. They didn't like Mrs. Weird either.

"That Weird woman thinks she's too good to be working in a factory,"

said one of the men.

"Acts like she's above us. Who the hell does she think she is?—The Queen?"

Then he laughed,

14

"Ha! The Queen?"

While they were laughing the men were spraying stiffening fluids on ladies' hats to keep them hat-shaped and stop them from going floppy. The smell of the liquids made Mrs. Weird feel like throwing up. She had a splitting headache. The hat-making machines made horrible noises. Like earthquakes and volcanoes going off at the same time. There was nowhere in the factory to get away from it. Noise was everywhere. Earthquakes and volcanoes and men's voices everywhere. Mrs. Weird sat at a table with the other women, who were much older than she was.

"You know what they say?"
said one of the women.
" 'If you're born in Liddleton, you die in Liddleton.'
That saying is as old as the hills. And you know what?
It's true!"
Then she laughed,
"Ha! It's true!"

While they were laughing the women were sewing imported pink silk flowers onto the sides of hats. The woman carried on.
"You know I worked it out the other day. I've sewn 68,950 pink silk flowers onto hats. That's pretty good going if you ask me. 68,950 pink silk fuchsias. When I'm gone there'll still be 68,950 women walking round with my fuchsias on their heads. And that makes me feel good. Like my life's had a purpose. Know what I mean?"

"I hate hats. I don't want to make hats. I hate hats,"
cried Mrs. Weird and she threw her hat down, ran into the
bathroom and locked herself up inside. The factory manager
banged on the door.

"Come out of the bathroom, Mrs. Weird! Come out!
Come out! Come out of the bathroom!"

In the car on the way home Mrs. Weird just stared out the
window. When she spoke it was in a little quiet voice.

"I don't want to live in Liddleton anymore.
I don't want to spend my life making hats.
I don't want to spend all my time clearing up after people.
People who don't care about me.
I don't know what I want.
But I know I don't want this."

Mr. Weird didn't say anything. He just parked the car and
got out. He didn't even close the door behind him. Poor Mrs.
Weird, she sat all alone in the car. Tears were streaming down
her face. There was no one in the world who would just put
their arms around her. Tell her everything would be all right.

Meanwhile, at school Steven was being interviewed:

"Sit down, Steven,"
said Mr. Whitlock.

"Now have you any idea what you want to do when you
leave school?"

16

"Yes, Mr. Whitlock."

"What, Steven?"

"I'm going to be a legend."

"What's that?"

"It's a superstar that people never forget."

"I see. Well, you'll be the only legend living in Liddleton."

"I'm not going to live in Liddleton, Mr. Whitlock.
I'm going to live in America.
All the legends live in America."

"Oh they do, do they, Steven?
And who in your estimation is a legend?"

"Judy Garland.
I'm going to be like Judy Garland."

"But Judy Garland is a woman, Steven."

"I know she is."

"Steven, I think you should try accountancy."

"Why?"

"I just think you should.
Yes, accountancy would be fine."

"Accountancy,"
muttered Steven as he left the room.

"Accountancy! Yeeeuch!"

And as soon as he got home from school he ran up to his
room and started singing "Swanee."

"Swanee,
How I love ya,
How I love ya,
My dear old Swanee.
I'd give the world to be
Among the folks in *D.I.X.*"

"*I* can't hear myself think,"

Mrs. Weird cried.

"I'm thinking but I can't tell what's on my mind!
I just want a bit of peace.
Is that too much to ask?
I can't stand that woman's voice."

Steven opened up his door.

"She's a legend. You don't understand.
I'm going to be a legend too."

"You'll never be a legend.
You've had no tragedy.
Do your homework."

Steven slammed his door. Mrs. Weird kept going.

"Don't you two know how to hang up clothes?
Don't you know how to wash a cup?
Don't you ever think of lifting a finger for me?
Why can't I have a home like ordinary people?
Why do I have to have a pigsty?
Other people's families aren't like this family.
Why can't I have a family like other people?
Why can't I have a lovely home like other people?
Why don't you talk to me instead of not saying anything?

Why don't you talk to me instead of always walking
away?
Why don't you do anything to help me?
Why won't you help me?"

Mr. Weird didn't say anything. He just walked out of the
house, got in his car and drove away.

"I got ravioli for dinner. Don't go.
I got ravioli. I bought ravioli.
You'll be sorry when I'm gone!"

Mr. Weird sat in a bar drinking wine, smoking cigarettes and
munching on Valium. When they asked him to leave he could
hardly walk. But he didn't worry about driving home and
crashing in his car because he had this theory that the car
knew the way and could drive itself home.

When he got in Mrs. Weird was fast asleep. She was so used
to him getting into bed in the middle of the night that she
never woke up. In the morning he managed to slip out of the
house without disturbing her, and he drove to the hat factory
because he had to meet his father there early. Well, when he
arrived Grandfather Weird was in one of his moods.

"You were supposed to be here ten minutes ago.
I have been waiting for you for ten minutes.
When will you learn, time is money. Time is money."

Mr. Weird got nervous as soon as his father opened his mouth,
and his fingers began to shake. So he swallowed a Valium.

19

"You didn't oil the machinery last night. I told you
to oil the machinery. Last night I said, 'These Italian
machines are precious objects.' What did I say last
night? I said, 'Precious objects.' I said, 'You clean
the machinery. You oil the Italian machines. Every
night. You care for them like children. They need
attention. They're worth a lot to me.' What did I say
last night? 'Precious objects. The Italian machines.
Oil them. They're children.' What do you do? What
did I say? 'They're worth a lot to me.' We're the only
factory in Liddleton with Italian machines. So you
oil them. Idiot! Oil and clean the Italian machines.
Every night. Oil and clean the Italian machines. Oil
and clean the Italian machines. Oil and clean the
Italian machines. So why didn't you do it?—Because
you're an idiot! Why did you do this to me, God?
Why did you give me an idiot for a son?"

Mr. Weird didn't say anything. He just walked out of the
factory. Got back in his car and drove home.

"Come back here. I want you back here!"

When he got in the house Mrs. Weird was in the bathroom.
He stood outside the bathroom on the landing next to a glass
table with a blue china vase and a marble ashtray on top of
it. For a long time Mrs. Weird didn't speak and when she did
it was in a little quiet voice.

"There's an oven full of ruined ravioli.
It's too ruined to reheat. So you'd better throw it out.
I'm going away. But I don't know where I'm going.
So you won't be able to write me there. Or call me there.

20

But I'm going somewhere. I'm getting away.
I'm going to get away.
Jesus Christ, there's even birdseed in the bathroom."

"Shut up!"

Mr. Weird picked up the marble ashtray, and hit Mrs. Weird and he hit and hit her, and every time he hit her he'd say,

"Shut up! Shut up! Shut up! Shut up! My whole life I've never done what I wanted. If it wasn't you nagging me it was my mother. Nag! Nag! You never stop nagging me. I can't do anything right. You always find something wrong. You've always got to get at me for something. I never wanted to work in a factory. I wanted to work on a farm. But I had my father pressuring me all the time. 'Work in the factory. More money in the factory.' I felt like saying to him, 'Fuck the money. I don't want the money.' Ever since I was born. No one wanted me. My parents didn't want me. You know what my mother said to me? She took me to one side when I was fifteen and she said, 'I must be honest with you. It's been on my conscience ever since you were born. We didn't want children. We didn't want you.' Then you know what she said? She said, 'I feel better now for telling you.' They didn't want me and you didn't want me. When did you ever want me? When? You didn't want me. Did you? Did you?

I want somebody to want me. I'm not an idiot."

And he ran down the stairs and out the front door. The men clearing the garbage called the police because there was a man

21

sitting on the front grass of one of the houses with blood all over his working clothes.

Steven came out of his room, into the bathroom, and he looked at his mother who was all crumpled up against the bath and he sighed,

"She always looks so unhappy.
Even when there's nothing to be unhappy about."

And he closed the door and went into his bedroom and put on his records and began to sing. And he thought to himself, "My voice is getting better and better." And he sang. Louder than he'd ever sung before. So loud that he didn't hear the police cars. And he didn't hear the ambulance. And he didn't hear the reporters. He didn't even hear them.

"With my high starch collar
And my high top shoes
And my hair piled high upon my head,
I went to lose a jolly hour on the trolley
And lost my heart instead.
With his light brown derby . . ."

2

SWAGGER

Steven at 16

Steven standing next to the River Thames in London at night, chewing gum

Inadvertent. That's what it was. That would be the word I would use to describe it. Chewing gum. That too. That had something maybe. That was in there. There's something happens when I chew gum. Some change comes about. A swagger. That's what it is. I swagger when I chew gum.

King's Road, Chelsea. It was very late. I was not drunk. I'd had beer but I was not intoxicated. Not by any means. Still, as some sort of safety precaution should I be stopped by some ambitious officer of the law and should he smell my breath and consider me disorderly, I was chewing gum. I was swaggering along King's Road. Checking cars. When all of a sudden this blue Mercedes slows down. Passes. But as I look at this blue Mercedes I perchance my eyes happen to meet the eyes of this blue Mercedes driver. Inadvertently a direct contact was made. Well, this car slows right down. Front door swings open. This guy leans out.—"Can I drive you anywhere?" My first thought was "I've never been in a Mercedes-Benz. I would love to be driven in a Mercedes-Benz." So in I get. We start driving. "What have you been doing?" this guy says. "Just walking," I says. The chewing gum is still in the mouth you understand. The words as they came out had a definite swaggering quality. "Do you want to go for a little drive?" he says. So we drive. Now this car makes no sound. I'm thinking at this point, "This is a silent car. Barely a purr. These cars are indeed worth the money you pay," when this guy puts his hand on my leg. At first I didn't say nothing. I don't know why but for some reason I didn't react. Then his hand moved up my leg. Still I said nothing. I just carried on chewing. Then he pushes his hand down between my legs. "I think you've gone far enough!" I says. "I'll give you money," he says, "I'll give you fifteen pounds. I just want to hold your hand. Here's fifteen pounds. I'll find a place to park. I won't hurt you." So I put the money in my pocket. Without thinking. Inadvertent. Just doing it. We're parked in a Chelsea mews. Just sitting there. Holding hands. Not saying anything. Just holding hands. And I look through one of the windows of one of the mews houses and there's this party going on. Big chandeliers. Oil paintings on the walls. All these college kids carrying on. It's just another world.

So this guy gives me his card. NORMAN PETERS. Executive Director. Trowbridge Plastics Incorporated. Says promise me

I perchance my eyes happen to meet the eyes of this blue Mercedes
driver. Inadvertently a direct contact was made.

you'll call. Well, I'm thinking, fifteen pounds for holding hands! It's real easy money. No skin off my nose. So I call his office. Put on a posh voice.

"Hello, can I speak to Mr. Peters? Hello, Mr. Peters. This is your friend from the other night speaking. I was wondering if you would be at all interested in us getting together again. I will be taking an evening promenade along King's Road. Twelve o'clock to-night. Should you be at all inclined. Same arrange-ment as before, Mr. Peters. Exactly the same."

So come twelve o'clock I'm strolling, ambling along King's Road, when along comes the blue Mercedes. Front door swings open. In I get.

"Hello, Mr. Peters."

"You didn't tell me your name."

"My name's Kevin."

Now, my name's not Kevin but I always wanted it to be. Every since I was a kid I wanted to be a Kevin. Now I am. Now I'm a Kevin.

"Kevin,"
says Mr. Peters.

"That's a nice name—Kevin. Very nice. A friendly name."

"Do you want some chewing gum, Mr. Peters?"

26

"No, thank you. I thought we'd drive to the airport.
Not Heathrow but a small runway on the outskirts.
It's closed down now. No longer in operation.
We won't be disturbed there. No people.
Just open country. Fields. Trees. Fresh air."

So we drive to this airport. Park near the runway.

"Kevin, let's get out of the car,"
he says.

"All right. It's a lovely night isn't it?"
I says.

"Look at the moon. It's full. I've never seen such a
huge moon."

"Kevin, I've been a naughty boy."

"Oh?"

"I've been fiddling the company. You're the chair-
man of the company, Kevin. You know what I've
been doing. You know what I've been up to and
you're gonna give me a lesson I won't forget. You're
really gonna give it to me. I may shout. Kick up a
fuss. Say you can't do this to me. But you're gonna
do it to me anyway. Because you're the boss, Kevin.
You're the one in charge. You do what you want to
do."

27

*　　*　　*

And so it began. I never hung out at Piccadilly or Leicester Square. None of the obvious places. I used to go to the cartoon cinema at Victoria Station. Never took long to find somebody at the cartoon cinema. It was like home turf. Soon as the cartoons began people would get up. Start moving around. There was no beating around the bush at the cartoon cinema. The guy at the door had no idea what I was up to.

"You really like cartoons,"

he'd say.

"You practically live here."

There was a few people I'd see on a regular basis. This guy called Christos. To Christos I was Steve.

"Oh, Steve,"

he'd say,

"When my wife leave me she continually send me toy rats through the mail."

And he'd laugh so hard he'd have to lay down. He was a photographer. *Vogue* magazine. Cooked lamb chops in sugar. Gave me weird Greek drinks. Said he was going to buy an island off Greece and just take pictures of blades of grass. His bathroom was all mirrors. You could see yourself from every angle. It was the first time I'd seen what I looked like from the side. For weeks I was bothered because I didn't think I looked like that.

28

There was an antique dealer in Pimlico. Used to drive me to this garage he used as a storehouse. Full of porcelain tramps sitting on benches. Old furniture. This big blue Jesus in the corner praying. I never did anything. He did it all. When it was over he'd drive me back to the cartoon cinema. He never spoke.

There was an architect. Collected animal heads.

"Shall we go into the rodent room?"

he'd say. And we'd go into the rodent room. All these squirrel heads poking off the wall.

At one point I thought I should stop doing it. Should get a regular job. Saw this position going working backstage on the musical *Annie*. The job was to supervise the orphans before the show. I thought, "Oh, that'll be all right." But these were not pleasant children. Made me very uneasy. Wouldn't do anything I said. They ran circles 'round me. It was horrifying. I'd dread going to the theater. Then I remembered this helium voice I used to do as a kid. Made the other kids laugh. Thought "I'll talk to them in that voice." So I went in one night and I stood there in front of them and they were carrying on. Ignoring me as usual and I said in this helium voice,

"Hello, everybody. Are we going to behave?
Are we going to do what we're told?"

Well the kids laughed and said, "Yes." So I did the voice and they were all right. Then I hear the orchestra starting up "It's a Hard Knock Life." So I say to the kids,

29

"All right, now go on the stage."
But the kids say,
    "No, do the voice."
So I said,
    "Get on the stage."
They said,
    "No, do the voice."
So I said in the helium voice,
    "Get on the stage."
They went,
    "Ha ha ha ha. Do it again."
I said,
    "Get on the stage!"

    "Ha ha ha ha. Do it again."

    "Get on the stage. Get on the fucking stage!"

It was a stupid show anyway. I ended up back in the rodent room.

    "What breed of squirrel is that?"

For some reason the money mounted up. I bought a truck. A '68 Bedford. Big black rusty thing in awful shape. Knew I was being taken for a ride. I took it anyways. Kept the Bedford in Victoria.

It was the middle of the night. I woke with a start. Out the window the sky was black. Raining buckets. Every time cars passed the road sizzled. I ran through the weather. To Victoria. To the truck. Got in and just drove. Not knowing where to. I just went. 'Long nearly deserted motorways. Not a soul in sight. Just rain clouds and lightning. Wipers moving left to right. Ended up at the coast. Herne Bay.

The oceanfront was wrecked. Stores broken in by the wind. An electrical place had its roof torn off. It was raining inside the store. Pouring down on stereos. There were TVs up in flames. A candy stand blew into an amusement arcade. This huge billboard of Petula Clark was slapping against a wall. Every time it hit Petula would crack. I stood on the shore. Eyes out to sea. Toward the pier. The water was going wild. Rearing up. Whole waves would leave the sea. Land on the pier. Huge pieces of water in midair. I thought my imagination had finally run away with me. The pier began to move. Shifted. Edged to one side. Like there was something underneath pulling it under. Some huge force that no one had made allowances for. The pier screamed and leaned into the waves. Screamed and submerged at the same time.

A flock of silver birds was flying low across the sand. The wind caught the birds. Blew them in my direction. The whole flock came crashing into me. But instead of bouncing off they went in. My body was full of birds. They were flying around inside me. Along my arms. Through my hands. Forcing me to dance.

When the sea had calmed I was still on the beach. The police came to see the damage. They saw me. Started poking fun,

"What the hell is that kid doing?"

I yelled from the top of my lungs,

"I can't stop dancing. My body's full of little birds."

My dad's been put away. He's under lock and key. I used to visit him all the time. Whichever prison they put him in. I'd get on a train. Not tell a soul where I was going. Just sneak off to see him with packs of cigarettes. Wearing this awful jacket he liked me in. So he wouldn't think I was letting myself go. Gets you nowhere. Just upsets. Him sitting there behind a piece of glass saying the same things over and over. Always repeating himself. Always the same.

"When I get out I'm going to buy that farm and we're gonna raise chickens and vegetables. We'll get dogs. Two dogs. German short-haired pointers. Bitches. Always get bitches. Bitches are brighter. Males go sluggish with age.

You know, I've been thinking, boy.

I should never have had children.

I can't even look after myself."

I love the river. Come here every day. Something about it— the river. The factories. The light on the water. The way cities look at night. I love cities.

One time I stood by the river the whole night. When the light came up the sky was red. It reflected in the water. Turned the water red. Everywhere you looked was red. Saw a man floating on the river. He was wearing one of those business suits that make everybody look the same. Arms out like a glider. Briefcase in his hand. Not making waves. Just moving away. I never saw mention anywhere. In the press. On TV. Not a word spoken. He just slipped out. On the sly.

People come up to you by the river. Strike up conversations. You find yourself just remembering things to perfect strangers.

"When I was a kid I used to watch these little falcons. Kestrels. At the back of our house there were fields. Bean fields and hills. A series of hills. Beyond the hills was a valley. In the valley was all mustard plants. Yellow for miles. I'd lay on my back in the mustard and watch kestrels. I could never understand how they just suspended themselves in the sky. They didn't seem to do anything. They didn't flap around. They just stayed up there. I found this relaxing.

Sometimes I'd fall asleep in the field. When I'd wake up, my toes would be clenched. Heart trembling in my chest. I'd look straight up. The kestrel would be over me. Suspended in the sky. Seemed so incredible. Everything else immediately reduced to insignificance. My feet would relax. Heart stop trembling.

One time I had this fear that the kestrel would be over me and suddenly decide to take a bowel movement. With the velocity and from that height, I'd be killed instantly. Murdered by an excretion. Could see all the police milling around me in the field.

"Here's the murder weapon, officer.

Looks to me like a bird dropping.
It is!
The suspect is a bird of prey."

I always had this fascination for things that could fly. Things that could just move around in the sky without holding on to anything.

Some birds move the whole way 'round the world. That kind of freedom. To just go wherever you wanted. And if you got tired of where you were you'd just go back up into the sky. Find somewhere else.

I've always envied birds.

3

WELCOME TO AMERICA

Steven at 20

On board an airplane

I was flying through the sky.
In a Freddie Laker plane.
I was thinking to myself,

"I'm never gonna go back to that country again."

I had one small bag with me.
It contained a selection of my favorite clothes.
I was looking out the window.
I had my little Olympus in my hand.
I was taking snapshots
Of clouds.

A tall lady in a uniform was renting headsets.
She had little bird wings on her shoulders
and *Laker Airways* written on her breasts.
She reminded me of Karen Black in *Airport '75*
and I thought,

"Wonder if she could land a skytrain?"

I gave her three dollars and she gave me a headset.
So I plugged myself into the armrest and I got
John Denver in my head,
and he was saying,
"*Take Me Home Country Roads.*"

Then Karen Black came back and she said,

"Would you like crabs?
Or would you prefer the beef?"

and I said,

"I don't eat meat."

And she swiveled around and produced a plate of food
specifically for people who don't eat animals.
I'm not sure what it was but it was very colorful.
When I had finished, she took away the tray and she said,

"Was that okay?"

and I said,

"What was it?"

and she said,

"Reality is something you rise above.
That's why I work up here in the sky."

36

I recognize those eyes.
The way that mouth moves.
Those ill-fitting teeth.

Then the lights went out and little screens came down.
And on the little screens was a little movie about a mountain
climber who sings.
A singing mountain climber.
Every time he climbed a new mountain he'd sing about it,
and I thought,

> "Mmmm, unusual film.
> I recognize those eyes.
> The way that mouth moves.
> Those ill-fitting teeth.
> That's no mountain climber.
> That's me.
> But that's not my voice.
> I've been dubbed!"

I shouted to the woman next to me,

> "I've been dubbed!"

But the woman leaned across and said,

> "That's your voice honey.
> It's just that you've never heard it before.
> It'll take some getting used to.
> It's a funny voice.
> Don't ever be afraid of your funny voice."

Then the other passengers started singing along. Singing along
with the screen. The whole flight in harmony. It's just like
when my grandmother used to go on coach trips to the Cots-
wolds. Out of the blue she'd start singing "Onward, Christian
Soldiers." I'd get embarrassed, but everybody on the coach
would sing along and unite and love each other. My grandmother's singing made people forget for a moment that they
were full of fear and distrust. Now my singing's doing the

same thing. And I looked out the window and there was this huge flock of Carolina wood duck. I shouted to the woman next to me,

> "Look wood duck!
> You don't get wood duck in Europe.
> Wood duck are American birds.
> Birds of North America.
> I've shifted continents.
> I'm in another stratosphere."

And the wood duck were looking at us because they'd never seen a plane full of singing people.
And I leap to my feet and I start yelling,

> "I'm gonna take my life in my hands and shake it and shake. Till all the bad parts fall out. Till they've all dropped out of me. Like dead leaves shaken from a living tree. There they go. All those rotting leaves. There they go. I'll shake and shake till only the living, the present, the alive is left. No dead leaves. No past. I'll shake off the past. Let the past get past. Let the past get past."

Then I realize, I'm saying what I feel.
Doing what I want. I get nervous again.
I'm afraid of what I might want to do.
I'm scared of what'll come out of my mouth.
But I can't stop. I'm being taken over by me!
The me I haven't been yet.
The me I'm going to be when I start being myself.
The frightened. The angry. The me that got buried in the childhood.
All of the me's are all out at once.
All acting and singing, asserting, saying,

39

"Let's see where the future can go!
Let's see where the future can go!"

Then applause. Cheers. Clapping passengers.

I'm a hit.

Karen Black comes out of the cockpit and she says,
"I don't know about you guys but I'm
just about ready to hit the ground.
Safety belts belted?
Extinguished cigarettes?
Luggage where it should be?
We're coming in to land.
Any minute now.
We're gonna be landing."

Build yourself a life and live with it!

"Coming in to land.
Any minute now.
Coming in to land.
Any minute now.
Coming in to land.
Any minute
Now.

Welcome to America."

The Redthroats was first presented at Performance Space 122 in New York City in May 1986. It subsequently reopened Off Broadway at the Second Stage in June 1987.

The lighting was designed by Carol McDowell. The production was stage-managed by Sabrina Hamilton.

Following the run at the Second Stage, *The Redthroats* was presented at Hallwall's, Buffalo, New York; Pyramid Arts Center, Rochester, New York; Procter's Too, Schenectady, New York; Clemens Center, Elmira, New York; The ICA Theater, Boston; Milwaukee Art Museum, Milwaukee; Life on the Water, San Francisco; Sushi Inc., San Diego; The Studio Theater, Washington, D.C.; Wadsworth Athenaeum, Hartford, Connecticut; Nexus Theater, Atlanta; The Goodman Studio Theater, Chicago; and the Mark Taper Forum (Taper Too), Los Angeles.

SMOOCH MUSIC

For John Colin

A NOTE ON THE PERFORMANCE OF SMOOCH MUSIC

Smooch Music is performed with a live jazz trio. The instruments used include saxophones, clarinet, vibes, acoustic bass and percussion. Only three sections of the piece—The Belter, The Love Club and They Went Their Separate Ways—are performed without music.

THE BELTER

In blackout

An English talent show in the East End of London. The M.C. has a thick Cockney accent.

M.C: Good evening, ladies and gentlemen, and welcome to the Black Horse Public House, Walthamstow. As you know Sunday night at the pub is Talent Contest Night, in which all the local talents come to show theirs off. So to speak. And starting off tonight we've got someone who may not be a big talent yet but he certainly is a tall talent. Come here, son.

Now, this young man's gonna sing for us. He is what's known in the business as a belter. That's someone who belts a song. Shirley Bassey is a belter. Tom Jones is a belter. Come to think of it Wales has produced a lot of our best belters. Well, what are you gonna belt for us tonight son?

CONTESTANT: I'm gonna do "Taking a Chance on Love."

M.C.:   He's gonna do "Taking a Chance on Love"! Lovely tune. Well I'm sure there are quite a few people in the audience tonight who have themselves taken a chance. On more than one occasion. Am I right? Oh, lovely crowd tonight, son. All right everybody I want you to give a big Black Horse hand to a young man who's taking a chance on love.

CONTESTANT: "Here I go again,
I hear those trumpets blow again,
I'm all aglow again,
Taking a chance on love.
Here I smile again,
I'm gonna run a mile again,
I'm in style again,
Taking a cha—"
I did it wrong.
Can I start again?
Can I start over?

Lights come up

THE LOVE CLUB

The American host of a swingers' club.

"Hello, swingers! Boy do we have a special night in store for you! Tonight we're gonna be watching George Wessell and Marjorie Farley make out for the first time together. Now these two young people have never once explored the possibility of each other's bodies. So tonight's gonna be real special for them. To do this we're gonna have to form a little circle around them. Circle, everybody. Circle. Now Marjorie's husband has never seen her with another man. So tonight's gonna be real special for him also. Are we nervous?—No, we're not nervous. Are we havin' a good time?—Hell, we're havin' a great time! And who made all this great time possible?

South Bay Shore Society Love Club. That's who. And who's
president of that great organization?—Me! What is the code
of our club? 'We are liberated. We are free. Our bodies belong
to each other. We deny no man or woman entrance to our
inner cores.' Now touch the genitalia of the person next to
you. Go ahead. Touch the genitalia! And repeat after me,
'There's no such thing as love. It's just a question of need.
There's no such thing as love. It's just a question of need.' "

ODESSA

The First Time

The first time I met you I thought you were somebody else.
The first time I talked to you it seemed like we'd known
    each other for a long time.
The first time I came up to your apartment I could tell
    you'd made an effort to look good.
The first time we kissed our teeth crashed.
The first time I saw you with no clothes on I couldn't
    believe my eyes.
The first time we made love the old lady from upstairs
    banged on the door and said,
        "Are you all right?"

51

On the way home after the first time I found myself
   thinking,
      "This is how it should be.
      No demands, just pleasurable sensations."

No Expectations

   I won't raise expectations.
   I won't raise expectations.
   I'm in a dancing mood.
   It's probably on account of you.
   I'm not going to think about it.

Unraveling

High-pitched voice

   It started at the Odessa.
   That's when I felt it begin to happen
   —the unraveling.
   The past, the present, what I wanted.
   All laid out.
   For you to decide.
   For you to pass judgment on.
   For you to decide if you wanted.
   If I was
   What it was,

52

> Whatever that was,
> You were looking for,
> For you.

Resistance

Deep voice

> It was in a dark room when you said it.
> When you said it there were no lights on.
>> "I don't know why I'm resisting you.
>> You're obviously a good thing for me.
>> I just can't give in.
>> I just can't relax with a good thing.
>> I've gotten used to unrequited love.
>> I'm comfortable with it.
>> Whenever there's a chance that love
>> may be given back,
>> I back away.
>> I get bratty.
>> I tease and torment.
>> You won't know what's happening.
>> It's just intimacy.
>> Intimacy scares the hell out of me.
>> Don't take it personally."

Isn't It Lovely?

But isn't it lovely
when everything's right,
when the kisses connect
and our legs are entwined?
Isn't it fine
when we open up,
put our defenses down?

Isn't it lovely
just watching TV,
eating ice cream,
not necessarily saying anything to each other.
Isn't it lovely?

Oh sometimes I wake myself up
in the middle of the night
just to watch you sleep.
And I press my chest against your back.
Breathe in sync with you.
The way you cover your face with your hand.
One time I woke up and you had
your mouth against my ear.
You were breathing into my ear.
And for a minute
I thought it was the sea.
Isn't it lovely?

Isn't it lovely just to go for a walk
in the neighborhood?
Who'd guess the simple pleasures
could feel this good?

And I press my chest against your back.
Breathe in sync with you.

Isn't it lovely?
Isn't it lovely?
Isn't this lovely?

And you said,
    "Where did you steal that from?
    A Hallmark card?"

They Went Their Separate Ways

They sat in a restaurant. The woman was distracted. The man said, "I think I'm in love with you. I know you're not in love with me. I don't expect you to say anything. I just wanted you to know. I just wanted to tell you." The woman was uncomfortable. She knew this was coming, still she didn't know what to say when it came. So she said, "Thank you. I hope it doesn't get in your way." That was something somebody had said to her. As they left the restaurant she said, "Do you mind if I spend the night on my own tonight?" He said, "Okay." She kissed him. They went their separate ways.

Well, the man thought, time is the key. Given time she'll come 'round. Maybe she's testing me. But as time went on the situation just became more strained because the closer they came the further she moved away and the man couldn't understand this because they seemed ideal. Twins of spirit. In fact they were so similar to each other that sometimes he got the impression he was talking to himself.

One night he came home and she was in the bath. With no lights on. She said, "I don't know what it means—love. I feel

56

like a ghost. I feel nothing." And he climbed into the bath water. Fully clothed. Held her. Felt so much his whole body shook. And she tried to love him. She really tried. But the closer they came the further she moved away.

Then she went away and the man was devastated. He couldn't believe the woman could do this, but he found somebody else almost immediately. But he treated the second woman just as the first had treated him. The closer they came, the further he moved away. And the second woman couldn't understand this because they seemed ideal. Like twins. In fact they were so similar to each other that sometimes the second woman got the impression she was talking to herself.

They sat in a restaurant. The man was distracted. The woman said, "I think I'm in love with you. I know you're not in love with me. I don't expect you to say anything. I just wanted you to know. I just wanted to tell you." The man was uncomfortable. He knew this was coming, still he didn't know what to say when it came. So he said, "Thank you. I hope it doesn't get in your way." That was something somebody had said to him. As they left the restaurant he said, "Do you mind if I spend the night on my own tonight?" She said, "Okay." He kissed her. They went their separate ways.

THE PINK TUTU

There's this kid who you sometimes see on the Lower East Side. But only in the summertime. And he's always wearing a pink tutu. And he's always dancing. And sometimes he'll be yelling,

"It's not me dancing.
It's the dress that's dancing!"

DRIVING

She kept having the same dream over and over in which she was in the back seat of a car being driven by a woman who didn't speak. Who didn't need sleep. Who'd just drive. And she'd be in the back. Looking out at the moving landscape. And sometimes in the dream she'd fall asleep. And when she'd wake up she'd look out the window and she'd be in a different state entirely.

THE BREAST

I was walking on Tenth Street. Mid-day. It was pouring rain. I was under an umbrella with my head looking down when I noticed a Polaroid snapshot lying on the sidewalk of someone's breast. I picked the breast up. It was wet. I had a pack of Kleenex in my pocket so I wiped the breast with a tissue. I was standing on the street looking at the breast when this guy comes up to me and says,

"Excuse me but I think that's mine."

YOU BRING OUT
THE ANIMAL

There's a lot of places that I've never been to.
Arizona for example.
The Serengeti.
There's a lot of wild animals in these places.
Jaguars. Polar bears. Big cats.
You know the type.
Press the right button and a machine can move forward.
Make the right connections and you could find yourself
in the middle of one of these places. Face to face with
the wild, wild animals.

PART I

It was upstate New York.
I didn't know where I was.
You told me your name
but I couldn't remember it.
You said,
     "Wanna go skinny dipping?"
I thought you were kidding.
We were both a little drunk.
I would have agreed to anything.
The sky was pitch-black.
The only light was the moon.
You said,
     "If we stick to this track we'll be there soon."
There was a fog hanging over the water.
Around the lake you could see the silhouettes of geese.
Graylag geese.
We took off all our clothes.
I stood in the freezing water up to my knees.
Something was tickling my legs.
You said,
     "Don't worry. It's the trout.
     They're only nibbling the hairs."
You came closer.
I went deeper.
The large gray geese moved into the water.
I could feel the trout swimming between my legs.
You stared into my eyes for the longest time.
Then you put your hand on my face.
Moved your hand around my face.
The mist was moving slowly across the water.
The large gray geese were floating away.

Clouds were moving away from the moon.
I said,
　　"What are you doing?"
You said,
　　"I'm healing you."

Part II

　　I'll be the putty in your hand.
　　I'll be the pawn in your game.
　　I'll be the son you never had.
　　I'll be the thing that makes you angry.

　　Roll me over.
　　Hear my heart going bang, bang, bang.
　　I just wanna lose control.
　　At least for an hour or two.

　　You can lift me up.
　　You can push me over.
　　Malicious and tender at the same time.
　　You can make me wonder what the hell I'm doing here.
　　I don't even like you.
　　But that doesn't matter.

　　I'll be the putty in your hand.
　　I'll be the pawn in your game.
　　I'll be the son you never had.
　　I'll be the thing that makes you angry.

　　Roll me over.
　　Hear my heart going bang, bang, bang.
　　I'm just trying to lose control.

PART III

It was in an apartment building.
On the Upper East Side.
He caught sight of what they were doing
in a full-length mirror
and it made him just want to go
further and further and further.
She said,
        "What are you trying to do?
You're hurting me.
Cut it out!
You're hurting me!"

PART IV

It was upstate New York.
It was still pitch-dark.
I was trying to find my way back to the cabin.
Something was running through the bushes.
Like a large animal.
But the animal had a flashlight.
You stood in a clearing ahead of me.
Threw the flashlight into a bush
and without saying anything
knelt down on all fours.
The ground was cold.
Your back was warm.
The wind blew through every part of me.
I looked up at the sky and the moon had moved.
I looked back down and part of my hand had disap-
    peared.

64

In the bracken and the bushes.
Under a clear black sky.
You gave me a taste of something it's hard to let go of.

Part V

It was in a railroad apartment on Avenue B.
He said,
>"You make it incredibly difficult for me to get out of
> bed.
>You make it incredibly hard for me to go to work.
>And I come home and you're laying on your stomach
>Pretending to be asleep.
>
>You bring out the animal.
>You bring out the animal.
>You bring out the animal.
>You bring out the animal."

THE ALLIGATOR

I hung around with this guy and when he laughed he looked like an alligator. I called it the real thing as soon as it started but it kept me suspicious. This man was very smart. We were inseparable. But every time he'd laugh I'd think, "He's just an alligator. Keep one step away."

So me and the alligator we'd go to movies and stuff and he was a pretty thing when he wasn't smiling. Why, he was the bee's knees when he wasn't smiling. But if ever I wanted to touch him he'd pull a face and make a growling noise. Grrrrrr! But still he'd call me up all the time.

Well, somehow me and the alligator we'd spend more and more time together. He'd go on about the way I lived. Giving reasons why I did such and such a thing. Explaining my past. Everything I did, he had a reason for. Even my wanting him he had some explanation why. Oh, he was really down on my whole way of life. Kicked up a lot of sneaking suspicions in me. Because he was usually right. Oh, he was a smart thing. I was very impressed by the alligator. I was impressed by his brains. His brains covered a broad range.

But I wanted him and he didn't particularly incline toward me and as you grow older you become less tolerant of that kind of thing.

So I started seeing other people. Lots of them. And it was all very pleasant. No pressure in sight. But still I'd visit the alligator. Oh, we'd laugh. Ha ha ha. But then I'd think, "But the alligator is the real thing. All the rest is just filler." But it would become problematic again and I'd be back at the movies or in a diner with the filler and that put back what the alligator took away.

Then one day the alligator met a woman. He called me up specially to tell me. He wasn't very sensitive.

"Oh, she's so smart,"
he said.

"She's so sweet. This is the real thing. You're just barking up the wrong trees all the time."

I didn't know what to say. But I stayed out of a whole area of town thinking I might run into the alligator when he was out on a date and get all upset and bent out of shape.

Then he started to get irritated by the woman. Analyzing her. Giving reasons why she did such and such a thing. Before

67

she knew what was happening, the alligator had turned her into a burden. Then he called me up and said he'd stopped seeing the woman and started seeing a man.

He called me up specially in the middle of the night. Just to tell me. He wasn't very sensitive.

"Oh, he's so smart,"

he said.

"He's so sweet. This is the real thing."

Oh, he was going on. I didn't know what to say. I just laid the phone down on the bed. The alligator was still talking. I could still hear his little voice muttering away and I went over to the mirror to try and see why I wasn't smart. Why I wasn't sweet. Why I couldn't be the real thing. Oh, I was giving myself a hard time. Then I don't know why but for some reason I decided to turn on the television. And on the television there's this actress and she's yelling at a photograph of an old man,

"If you'd have loved me as a child I wouldn't be this needy all the time! If you'd have shown me some affection. That I was worth something to you, I wouldn't be hurling myself at every Tom, Dick and Harry that walked through the door!"

And I'm looking at the actress and she's looking at me. And I pick up the phone and the alligator's still talking. I can still hear his little voice muttering away. And the actress is looking at me. And she's trying to cry. But she's not a very good actress.

So no tears are coming out.

TALKING TO YOU ON THE PHONE IS BETTER THAN BEING WITH YOU

I.

On the corner of Eighty-first Street and First Avenue there's a phone booth. Sometimes if you pass the phone booth at night the phone'll start ringing. Just as you're walking past it'll ring. And if you pick it up there'll be a woman's voice on the other end and she'll say,

> "Hi! My name's Honey.
> I just stepped out of the shower.
> I'm naked as a seashell.
> Drippin' everywhere.
> Wanna talk awhile?
> You want Honey to give you her number?

69

You wanna run home?
Call Honey from the comfort of your own home?
Or you wanna talk to Honey's friend Joe?
Joe'll do whatever you want on the phone.
You wanna j/o with Joe?
Or you wanna have a three-way with Honey and Joe?
Honey has two extensions in her apartment.
You can talk to both of us at once.
Or you wanna talk to Honey and Honey's friend Cathy?
Cathy can come over.
Two sexy girls at the same time.
Or you can talk to Honey and Cathy and Joe
and we can get Joe's friend Pedro to come
over and speak a little Spanish."

II.

They never actually talked to each other.
They'd just leave messages on each other's machines.
What with their schedules and everything.
It got to the point where he would avoid calling
if he thought she might be home.
But somehow the messages were becoming more inti-
    mate.
Getting more involved.
He would come in late at night and switch to
"Rewind Messages"
and listen to her voice coming out of the Phone Mate.
He found it relaxing.
The way she said, "Hi."
Comforting.
The sound of her voice could lift him up

70

after a bad day.
He'd turn off all the lights.
Take his shoes off.
Put his feet up on the couch
and play her messages back.
Over and over.

"Hi, it's me.
Guess who?
Yes, it's me again.
Guess who?
Shnoogums.
You'll never guess who this is."

THE RESCUE

Whispered

I had this dream in which the city was all frozen over. Ice over everything. Trees filled with snow. I was standing next to a very wide road. The air was white. There was a woman lying in the middle of the road. Lying face down. Cars were coming toward her. No one was running to help. She was half buried in snow. Barely visible. The cars wouldn't have noticed. She'd have been a bump in the road. I ran into the middle. Stood up straight over her body. The cars had to drive 'round me. I was too large to ignore. I dragged her through the snow. She was a very tall woman. Difficult to maneuver. There was a bench next to a bus stop by the road. I pulled her up on the bench. Her eyes had frozen closed. I had to put my hands on her eyes to melt them. Ice water ran down her face. I held my hand against her eyes. Something underneath the lids was quivering. Her eyes were melting. She opened them. Gave me a look. The like I've never seen before. An overwhelming look. It passed straight through me. I could feel the look inside me. Affecting me internally. I gave her the same look back. It was mutual. For one long moment. I didn't know where it was coming from. I'd never looked at anyone this way before. For one long moment. We couldn't take our eyes off each other. Then I woke up. Realized I was just dreaming. I tried to go back to sleep. To be with her again. To get her back. But I couldn't. I was way too wide awake. I couldn't get back.

THE SEX LIFE

When I was a kid. When no one was in the house. I would go over to the cupboard under the stairs and take out the vacuum cleaner. Plus all the attachments. I'd plug the vacuum cleaner into the wall. Attach the long metal tube to it. The one you add all the attachments to. Then I'd place the tube's hole against my neck. Switch the vacuum cleaner on with my foot. Hold the tube so it sucked my neck for about ten minutes. Then I'd change sides and repeat the whole operation. Then I would put the vacuum cleaner and the attachments back under the stairs. Go over to the mirror. And sure enough I'd have hickeys. Or lovebites as we used to call them. Then I would go out and meet my friends and pretend nothing had happened. Pretty soon they'd notice the marks on my neck and they'd say,

74

"He's had sex again! How does he do it?
What's his secret?"
And I'd give them a knowing look and not say anything.

Then we'd go and look at the *H & E* magazines. *H & E* was this magazine specially for nudists. The H & E part stood for Health and Efficiency. It was full of pictures of nude families playing volleyball. In special camps where people who didn't want to wear clothes could go and just take them off.

There'd be a sentence under each photograph: "Here's Christopher. Age 6. Nude. Playing gin rummy with his Aunt Trixie. Age 47. Two people enjoying their nudity." Nude aunts. Nude uncles. Nude nephews. Nude nieces. All these nude grandmothers sitting round campfires eating chickens.

You didn't have to be a certain age to buy *H & E* because it was officially a health magazine. Anyone could buy it. The only trouble was most of the people in *H & E* were really overweight. They'd have big bellies that would hang low, so you couldn't really see anything.

Sometimes Kevin White would come and look at the *H & E*'s. Kevin White lived up the street. He was always trying to get me to do things. After a lot of persuasion Kevin convinced me that if I showed him mine he would show me his. This all happened behind the shed. Well it was a big success. So we started exposing ourselves to each other on a regular basis. Then I don't know what happened. It must have started to be too much for him 'cause after a while Kevin started playing hard to get. That ended that.

Then one day I was riding my bike in the countryside. I saw this package in a ditch. I jumped down and pulled it open.

It was full of magazines. Nude magazines. Real nude magazines. Not the *H & E* kind. All the magazines had their covers torn off. The women in the pictures looked really mean. Most of them had their tongues sticking out. There was a page where readers could send in photos of their wives and the magazine would print them. It was really peculiar. All the wives were wearing boots and holding bull whips. There was another section called "Erotic Tips: What You Can Do with Eggs."

It had instructions: "Lie in an empty bath.
Take a dozen raw eggs.
Crack the eggs over your body.
Then rub them in.
—A delightful erotic experience."

Suddenly this car started coming toward me. I was convinced it was the people who owned the magazines coming to get them back. Panic set it. I got back on my bike and sped off.

When I got home no one was in. I couldn't get my mind off the eggs. So I went to the refrigerator to see if we had any. We did. There were three dozen. At first I thought, "How many eggs can I take without anyone noticing that any are gone?" Then I must have forgotten about that because I ended up taking all of them up to the bathroom. I took off all my clothes and climbed into the empty bath. It was really cold against my back. Took a long time getting used to it. Then I started cracking the eggs over my body. They looked awful. The yolks were breaking and sliding off me. But nothing was happening. No delightful erotic experience. So I started in on the second carton. Then the third. By this point I was about

76

"He's had sex again! How does he do it?
What's his secret?"

six inches deep in eggs. Every time I moved a wave of eggs would wash up over my chest.

I was rubbing them in when something started to happen. So I kept rubbing them in. The eggs were splashing every-where. Sloshing over the side of the bath. There were eggs up the wall. I got egg in my eye. But something was hap-pening. Maybe I was having it. A delightful erotic experience. There were eggs everywhere. I didn't care.

Something was happening.

Something was definitely happening.

Something was happening.

Something was definitely happening.

Something was happening.

Something was definitely happening.

Then I realized,

THIS MUST BE WHAT ALL THE FUSS IS ABOUT!

DONNA SUMMER

"Someone has to push women off the precious
     pedestal you place them on,"
she said.
     "Women aren't like that.
     That's not what women are like,"
and kissed him on the mouth, pushed him up against his
own kitchen wall and pulled him down onto the carpet.

One kiss and she turned from being his best friend into some-
     thing else entirely and she wasn't prepared to make the
     transition gradually.
She wouldn't take no's.

She wouldn't listen to maybe's.
She had him by the Fruit of the Loom.

They rolled from the kitchen into the living room.
From the living room into the hallway.
From the hallway onto the bed.
He felt like he was in a movie or something.
She thought,

"I can't believe he's got his hand on my crotch.
It only took eighteen months to get it there."

He said,

"Just when you think you're one thing you realize you
could be something else."

That night he dreamt he went hang gliding with his mother.
He told her about the dream in the morning.
She didn't say anything.

She'd show up at his apartment at the oddest hours.
She never told him she was coming.
She always brought him flowers.
She showed him all the points of interest on a woman's ge-
ography.
A complete and guided tour of her own anatomy.
He found women a complete mystery.
He'd find himself just looking at her sometimes.

She'd say,

"Women aren't like that.
That's not what women are like.
Women aren't like that.
That's not what women are like."

She kept a diaphragm in his bathroom cupboard.
She gave the diaphragm a name.
She called it Donna Summer.
She'd say,

    "Slow down.

        I have to get Donna."

She told him about the affairs she'd had with other women.
It surprised her how little difference there was.

    "Smaller bones,"

she'd say.

    "That's the basic difference: smaller bones.
    Plus of course women know exactly where to go.
    There's none of that hit or miss, fiddling around.
    They just know.
    Exactly where to go."

She'd say,

    "Sometimes I really want a woman.
    Other times I feel like a man.
    Other times I'll take a Mark V Deluxe Wahl vibrator over
      both of them."

She loved to shock him.
He loved to shock her too.
They'd spend whole evenings just freaking each other out.
She made him feel extremely masculine.
Why sometimes it almost verged on macho.

She'd say,

    "Women aren't like that.
    That's not what women are like.

Women aren't like that.
That's not what women are like."

But he was too addicted to chaos to put up with ease and she
wouldn't put up with his inconsistencies. And for some reason not quite understood by either of them they didn't see
each other for a long time. And when they did he was with
somebody else and she took him to one side and said,

"Is that what you left me for?
Women aren't like that.
That's not what women are like."

And he looked at who he was with and there was no com-
parison.

And she lingered on his mind for the rest of the day. Like a
song you can't get off your head and he felt a sinking feeling
in his chest that he couldn't explain. And he couldn't understand how he could open up so easily and close the same
way and she kind of haunted him for the rest of the day.

When he got home he went over to the bathroom cupboard.
He still had her contact-lens fluid.
He still had that special soap she used
and he still had Donna Summer.

THE DREAM

Softly spoken American accent

I had this dream in which I was lying next to you. You were fast asleep. Your mouth a little way open. A small sound was coming out. In this dream I had been reduced in size to such an extent that I couldn't be seen. But I had this overwhelming desire to climb into you, move around inside you. So I did. I climbed across the pillow, up your neck, onto your chin. Moved on my hands and knees between your lips. The wind in your mouth made it difficult to stand. So I slid on my front along your teeth to the back. I stood up on your gums and dived down your throat. I was completely inside you. Moving around in you. Exploring areas of you that no one else had seen. Purple blood streams. Alimentary canals. Enormous cells filled with aspects of your personality which you never employ. These huge internal organs would shift and sway and sort of come toward me and then back off. The experience was truly liberating. I could feel it shaking off the rut I was in. All those doldrums just dropped away. In this dream I had a mission. To find your heart. Touch your heart. All the time I could hear it. I kept looking for a way and all the time it was within earshot but the harder I tried to reach the further away it seemed to get. Like it was running. Eventually it got too frustrating trying to connect. The wonder of being in incredible surroundings wore off. I became sick of only seeing you. I thought, Give up. Get out of here. But when I tried to leave I couldn't find the way out. I was caught up. Surrounded in you. When you spoke I couldn't get away from your words. Whatever you said affected me. I became physically hungry. This hunger would not go away but there was no food to eat. There was only you. The only thing to eat was you. So I started to eat. It kept me going but it made you sick. You couldn't understand why you were getting sick but it was me eating you away inside. I didn't mean to make you sick. It was just the situation.

THE SNAKE LADY

There used to be this lady who was always outside the Metropolitan Museum.
She always wore very heavy makeup and she always carried around this big Macy's bag.
Inside the Macy's bag she had a boa constrictor.
She would sit on a bench outside the museum and say to people,

"Give me a dollar and I'll kiss the snake."

There were always a lot of tourists around.
Anxious to get interesting pictures of New York.

So they would hand over their dollars.
When the money had all been collected the lady would whisper,

"Hey, baby. C'mon, baby. Who loves you?"

And the snake would rise up out of the Macy's bag and hover next to her lips. Then sure enough the two of them would kiss and the tourists would start snapping. Then another group would come along and she would repeat the whole operation. The only problem was the lady always wore heavy makeup. Every time the snake kissed her it got red lipstick on its face. The lipstick would accumulate after each kiss. There was a build-up. After three or four of these kissing sessions the snake's head was one big lump of lipstick.

Don't let your lover make a mess of you.

Don't let your lover make a mess of you.

DON'T LET YOUR LOVER MAKE A MESS OF YOU

Don't let your lover make a mess of you.
Don't let your lover make a mess of you.

If he or she starts lying to you.
Starts saying things you know aren't true.
Don't just sit there nodding your head.
Pretending you believe what he or she said.
Say,

"Hold on a minute.
Don't give me that.
I know you.
I know where you're at.
Don't give me that."

And if it happens repeatedly, leave.
But,

Don't let your lover make a mess of you.
Don't let your lover make a mess of you.

If he or she is seeing people on the sly
and that doesn't suit you, don't compromise.
Get wise.
If you've tried everything you know
To be their one and only and that don't work,
just let 'em go.
But,

Don't let your lover make a mess of you.
Don't let your lover make a mess of you.

I kept catching snippets of people's conversations.
Two girls passed me on the street.
One was in tears.
She was saying to the other girl,

"... and then he said,
'Would you be really upset if I told you
I wasn't a toreador from Mexico?' "

Don't let your lover make a mess of you.
Don't let your lover make a mess of you.

These two guys were talking in a coffee shop.
One of them looked at the other and said,

"... and then he said,
    'I think we should just be friends.'
I said,
    'I don't want to be friends. I've got friends.
    I want sex! What am I gonna do with more friends?' "

Don't let your lover make a mess of you.
Don't let your lover make a mess of you.

If he or she can't make up their minds about the way they
feel. Chances are they're not feeling what they should be
feeling. But are too scared or polite to say so. That's your cue
to take your records out of their record collection. Take your
toothbrush out of their toothbrush rack. Take the spare pair
of underwear you keep in their top drawer back. Pop them
into a plastic bag and head for the door. Saying,

    "When you've made up your mind give me a call.
    You've got the number."

But,

Don't let your lover make a mess of you.
Don't let your lover make a mess of you.
Don't let your lover make a mess of you.

You can always get another one.
Oh, you can always get another one.

WIRED AND CONNECTED

I was testing cantaloupes.
You were jogging on the street.
You looked at me.
I looked at you.
I got self-conscious.
I looked back down at fruit.
You looked around again.
I thought,

> "Am I gonna get beaten up?
> Or what?"

I paid for one large cantaloupe
and followed you just the same.

We got to a DON'T WALK sign.
I was straining to be cool
and you said,

> "I have to see a doctor. But I'll be finished at 2:00.
> And I would like to meet you here.
> If that's what you wanna do."

and I said,

> "Mmmmm."

And I went home
and I shaved my face
and I was there at 1:55.

We had a conversation in Central Park.
I started to think you were a fool.
By the time we got to Broadway
I'd changed my mind.
Several times.
You spoke to several people you knew:
A man selling ice cream.
A man from South America.
Said you lived with a TV producer
and I thought,

> "Ah-hah! A kept person."

Because you really were so good.
Just to look at.

On the floor of my studio we ate combination pizzas. You had attached to you a small object that reminded me of one of those fashionable, portable cassette recorders. It measured the irregular beats of your heart. They were testing them that day.

I kissed you.
Take-out pizza passed from mouth to mouth.
And I said,

> "Should I pull the bed out of the couch?
> Would that upset the heartbeat machine?"

Under your track suit were wires.
I held you.
Wiring in between.
There was a small green light on the heartbeat machine.
When I touched you the numbers moved faster.
And I said,

> "How are you going to explain this to the doctors?"

I kissed your face.
From the lashes to the lips.
We rolled like tongues.
While you were asleep
I made sure you were still plugged in.

At midnight you had to meet some man.
We put on clothes.
My hair was sticking up in all directions.
You moved across the room in a torn-off scarlet T-shirt.
And I thought,

> "You really are so good.
> Just to look at."

On the street outside a rich hotel there was a group of rich
people waiting for cabs. You stopped in the middle of them.
Kissed me on the mouth. It made someone wonder what the
hell was happening to this world. I left you on the corner of

Seventh Avenue and Fifty-eighth Street. I turned 'round half-
way down the street and you turned 'round at the same time.

Back in the bed I found a hair from a certain part of your
    body.
I put it into a brown envelope to keep.
Later that week I flew to California for ten days.
I flew back after three.

And I called your number.

And I called your number.

And I called your number.

And I called your number.

FALLING OVER MYSELF
TO GET TO YOU

In the middle of the morning
I want to break it off.
Then I see what I'm doing
and I change my mind.
You don't know what's happening.
Falling over myself to get to you.
Falling over myself to get to you.

You're not good-looking enough!
There's just no spark.
I can tell what we're gonna do.
Whether the lights are on
or we're in the dark.

Falling over myself to get to you.
Falling over myself to get to you.

You get used to things a certain way.
And when it's different.
Makes you uneasy.
Makes you nervous, doesn't it?
And your moods change like radio stations.
She says,

> "I don't want to hear this song.
> I don't want to hear this one again."

Falling over myself to get to you.
Falling over myself to get to you.

So you pull out the plug
and there's no sound at all.
And you go through the old motions.
But the old motions don't fit.
And you don't know what to do
because this is new.
She doesn't respond as you expect her to.
Because she's smarter than you!
But you close so tight that all you can think
when she touches is,

> "Please don't do that."

She says,

> "While the complicated emotions simplify,
> I'll be in the next room watching the paint dry."

On the way home someone gives you the eye.
You take it home with you.

What the hell am I doing?
Falling over myself to get to you.
Falling over myself to get to you.

So you run right back and you try to undo.
And you put some smooch music on the stereo
to go with the mood.
And she'll stand above you
and you'll feel like liquid.
And you want her to dive right in again.
But she's not a martyr.
She's not there to save you.
And when she touches you
the surface shivers.
Your eyes spill over
and it starts to feel true.
Then you wonder if it's coming from the music
or if it's coming from you.
Falling over myself to get to you.
Falling over myself to get to you.

And when she's away from you,
you sit around and brood.
About the consequences of.
The damage you do.
If the effects are irreparable this time.
When I'm out of my senses.
When I lose my cool.
Falling over myself to get to you.
Falling over myself to get to you.

HE MET HER ON A SUNDAY

When they got to her apartment he went straight for her record collection. Because he always believed you could tell a lot about a person by what they listened to. Well, she had lots of jazz and singers with soul. So he figured she was cool. She showed him her poetry and her Guatemalan clothes. She said she went to school in Jersey with Phoebe Snow. He felt curiously close to her. He felt curiously close.

The next day he got a call. She was down the street. And had he eaten dinner yet? And did he want to meet? Well, he had but he said he hadn't. So they grabbed some Szechuan. There were a lot of strange people in the restaurant. And he forgot that he was nervous and he forgot that he was shy and he leaned across the table and said, "Do you want to spend the night?"

She woke up early, like you do when you're sleeping in a strange place. Plus the garbage trucks outside made the windows shake. She waited for him to wake up to see how he'd react at seeing her next to him and when he opened his eyes . . . he started grinning.

And that was just the beginning.
Oh, that was just the beginning.

BABY IT'S YOU

I woke up with a strange taste in my mouth.
It was you.
While you were asleep
I used your shampoo.
It made me smell just like you.
While you were asleep
I went through your clothes.
I stole your T-shirt.
Wore it to work.
The people there were saying,

"Where did you get that T-shirt?
It really isn't you."

And I said,

100

"Yes it is."

But that wasn't true.
It wasn't me.
It was you.
While you were asleep
I had breakfast with my friend.
We got into an argument
and he said,

"Where did you get that attitude?"

I said it was new.
It wasn't new.
It was you.
Baby, it's you.
Baby, it's you.
If I had back-up singers they'd be going,

"Baby, it's you.
Baby, it's you."

But I don't.
Baby, it's you.
Oh,

"Here I go again.
I hear those trumpets blow.
I'm all aglow.
Taking a chance on love.
Taking a chance on love.
Taking a chance on love."

Smooch Music was first presented at The Kitchen in New York City in February 1987 after a work-in-progress showing at Performance Space 122 and the Bandshell in Central Park.

All original music was composed by Roy Nathanson, except "Baby It's You," music by Ed Tomney and Jonathan Borofsky. The lighting was designed by Carol McDowell. The sound was designed by Carl Lugus, the production was stage-managed by Lori E. Seid.

Smooch Music was performed with Roy Nathanson on tenor, alto, soprano saxophones and vibes. Bradley Jones on double bass. E. J. Rodriguez on drums and percussion.

Following the run at The Kitchen, *Smooch Music* was presented in Boston at the Institute of Contemporary Art.

ABOUT THE AUTHOR

David Cale was born and raised in England. He moved to New York in 1979. He has written and performed the shows Smooch Music *(in collaboration with composer Roy Nathanson) and* The Redthroats, *for which he received a Bessie Award for Outstanding Creative Achievement. His work has been presented throughout the U.S. He appeared in the H.B.O. television special "Bette Midler's Mondo Beyondo," and the films* Radio Days, *directed by Woody Allen, and* Moon Over Parador, *directed by Paul Mazursky.*